All About

Jason Momoa

Jason Momoa Biography Children's Book for Kids

(With Bonus! Coloring Pages and Videos)

By All About Books

Before You Go Any Further, Get Your FREE Gift! (Worth $67)

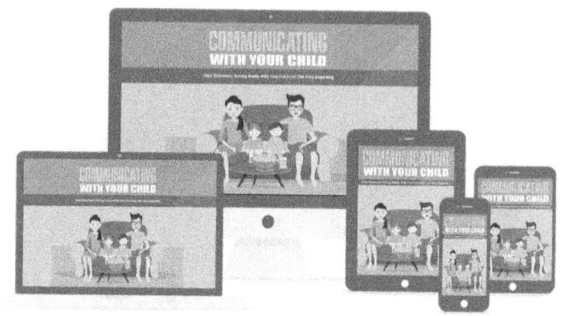

Never Fear "The Call" from the School or the Hospital Again!

How to Effectively Communicate With Your Child About *Safety* in a <u>Fun Way!</u>

Did you know if children are not taught properly about safety at a young age, it can potentially lead to reckless, dangerous behaviors even when they become a teenager or an adult?

Never fear "the call" from the school or the hospital with this comprehensive video course!

It'll teach you how to communicate effectively with your young ones about safety without boring them!

(Limited-Time FREE Gift)
Get It Before It Expires Here:

https://allaboutbookseries.com/freegift/

Table of Contents

Disclaimer and Note to Readers:

This book is an unofficial tribute book to Jason Momoa from a fan to support his legacy.

The information in this book is provided for educational and entertainment purposes only.

The information in this book has been compiled from reliable sources. It is accurate to the best of the author's knowledge; however, the author cannot guarantee its accuracy and validity and cannot be held liable for any errors or omissions.

If you use the information contained in this book, you agree that the author is free from and not liable for any damages, costs, and expenses, including any legal fees, potentially resulting from applying any of the information provided by this guide.

The disclaimer applies to any damages or injury caused by the use and application, whether directly or indirectly, of any advice or information presented, whether for breach of contract, tort, neglect, personal injury, criminal intent, or under any other cause of action. You agree to accept all risks of using the information presented inside this book.

If an individual cites this publication as the source of information, it does not imply that the author or publisher endorse the individual or organization's knowledge. This book is an unofficial fan tribute and has not been approved or endorsed by Jason Momoa or his associates.

Introduction to Jason Momoa

Jason Momoa is an American actor, writer, and filmmaker. He is famous for his role as Khal Drogo in the HBO series, *Game of Thrones*. He is also renowned for his role as Aquaman in the DC Extended Universe film *Aquaman*.

The forty-two-year-old actor was born in Hawaii but was raised in Norwalk, Iowa. He attended university in Hawaii so he could connect with his roots. He is 6 feet, 5 inches tall. Apart from his interesting movie roles, there are many exciting things about Jason Momoa.

Did you know that he is an avid rock climber?

He is a rock climber who also has his line of rock climbing products. He showcases his rock climbing on his YouTube channel. Rock climbing is not just a hobby for him; it's a sport. He also teaches his kids rock climbing.

As a way of helping the environment, Jason has a canned water business, "Mananalu." According to the company website, most plastics don't get recycled. They go into the ocean. However, most of the aluminum used globally has been in circulation for a while. When you dispose of it, it gets re-used. This business is not a surprise as his wife has mentioned that his biggest pet peeve is single-use plastics.

Jason is also very art-oriented. His friend and business partner, Brian Andrew Mendoza, mentioned that Jason loves art. They could be going out, and Jason would stop to take a picture of the sun. Jason is the son of a photographer, so it is no surprise that he is into cameras. Jason has a collection of Leica Cameras.

Jason is not just artistic; he loves his Harley Davidson motorcycles. He has quite the collection. He has '36, '37, and '39 knuckleheads. He loves vintage bikes. He also has a 1956 Panhead named Mabel after his grandmother. His bikes don't stop at vintage. He also has modern bikes. He has a 2020 LIVEWIRE; yes, it's an electric motorcycle, but Jason swears that he has made even the most hardcore bikers like this bike. He also has a 2021 Pan American. He really loves his Harley Davidson. He also has a BMW R Nine T Scrambler and a custom-made Vallkree Drifter Electric Motorbike in his collection. Jason's YouTube is filled with videos of him riding his motorbike.

Jason also loves his cars. He owns an Aston Martin DB5U and a pink Cadillac named Bernadette, which he has owned for fifteen years. He got his inspiration from Elvis. He also owns a Ford F-150 RV. Jason loves this Earth Roamer so much that he even took it to the premiere of Aquaman. He owns a white Range Rover, too. Jason also has a Land Rover Defender Series 3. He loves this car a lot. Jason sold it to finance a movie he was producing. He repurchased it from the buyer once he had the money.

Jason loves Guinness beer, and he has his own line. The bottle is designed with Jason's signature and his Hawaiian tattoo.

He plays the guitar and loves to share parts of his life with fans through his YouTube channel.

He is married to Lisa Bonet, and together, they have two children. Jason loves being a father. Growing up without one in his life, he struggles occasionally. He doesn't want to be the authoritarian dad, he wants to connect and be vulnerable with his children. He has a tattoo of their names over his heart. The script uses their childhood handwriting when they first learned to write their names.

Jason and Lisa have a combined net worth of $14 million.

Who is Jason Momoa?

http://allaboutbookseries.com/WhoisJasonMomoa

Jason Momoa's Early Childhood

Joseph Jason Namakaeha Momoa was born on August 1, 1979, In Hawaii to Coni Lemke, a photographer, and Joseph Momoa, a painter. His father is of native Hawaiian ancestry, while his mother has a mix of Pawnee of German and Irish origin.

His parents divorced when he was six months old. He moved to Iowa with his mom.

Jason has admitted that growing up with a single mother shaped his worldview. She opened his eyes to a world of art and music. She instilled a love for rock climbing and skateboarding in him.

Jason is a product of two opposing worlds.

As someone who was mixed race, Jason could never fit in. He was different from most kids in Norwalk, Iowa. He mentioned that "he was a little hippy kid from Iowa. I was no toughie; I spent my fair share of time stuffed in lockers." Being the only mixed-race kid in school, Jason was beaten a lot. When he got into art and skateboarding, the big guys in his town were against it; he was hit again. He was called a freak for wearing Birkenstocks in middle school.

Question to Ponder: How do you think Jason felt all the times he was beaten, stuffed in lockers, and called a freak?

Jason visited Hawaii often to meet his father and members of his extended family on the paternal side. He also found it challenging to fit in there. Many locals just saw him as a "Haole from the mainland." Jason's connection to the island kept getting stronger as he spent more time with his family.

Question to Ponder: Have you ever been in a situation where you didn't fit in with others no matter how you tried? How do you think a young Jason felt knowing he also didn't fit in with his paternal side of the family?

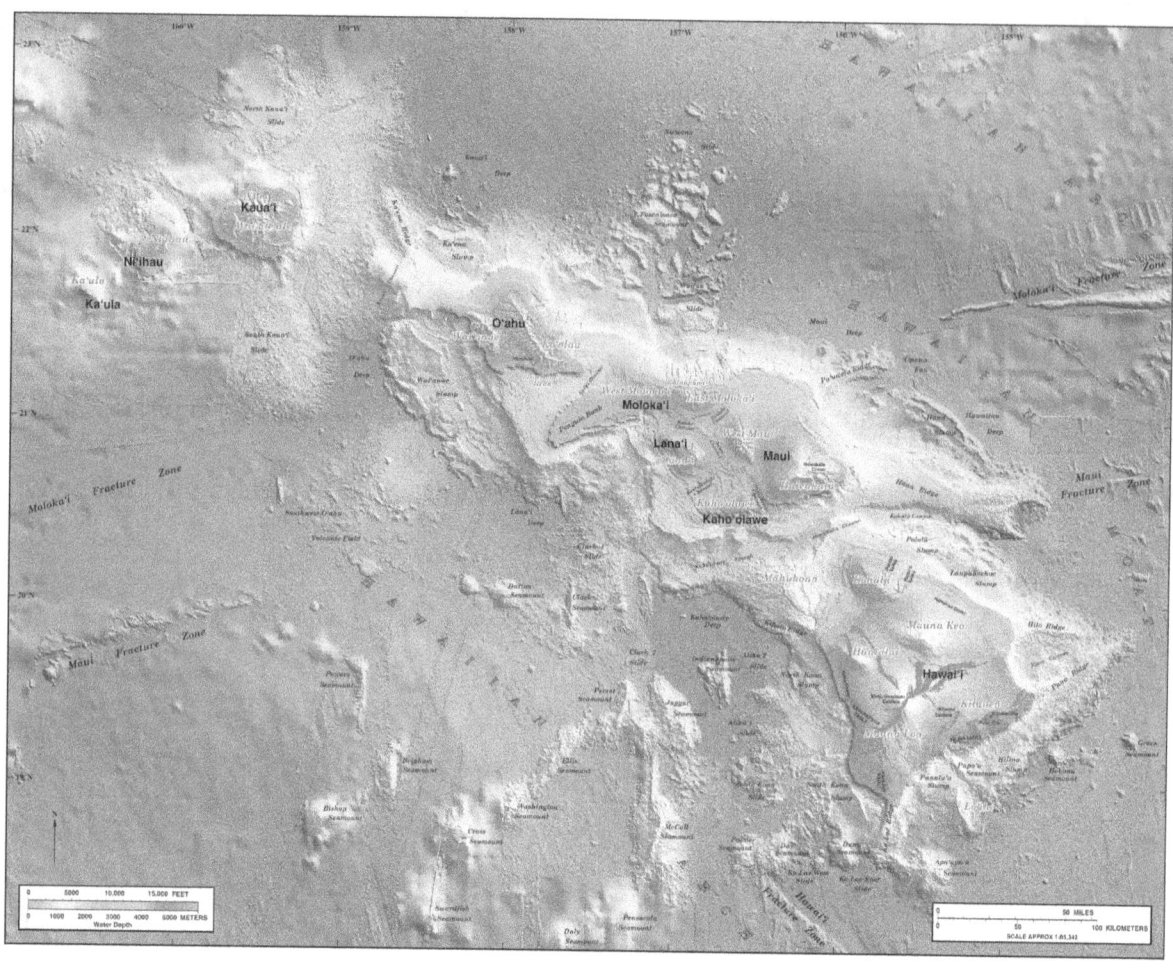

"Bathymetric map of the Hawaiian Islands" by USGS: Barry W. Eakins, Joel E. Robinson
Per USGS, Copyrights and Credits, this map is in the public domain (USGS work); no copyright
assertions by the non-government parties were made.

Early Career of Jason Momoa

Jason Momoa started working part-time at a surf shop in Hawaii when he was nineteen. At that time, he heard about casting for *Baywatch Hawaii*, so he and his cousins went to check it out. Jason claims that he and his cousins wanted to see the girls at the casting. There were many people; about 1300 people showed up for the audition. He was in the queue for seven hours before his turn. Jason got to the front of the queue; he was asked for his resume. He told the crew that he didn't have a resume. So, they asked him if he had acted before the audition. He said to them that he hadn't. They asked if he had ever done a modeling job; he replied yes, that he had modeled for Louis Vuitton and Gucci. He turned to his friend and casually mentioned that his friend did Prada. His friend replied in the affirmative, saying he did a shoot in Japan.

The modeling job was a lie, but the *Baywatch* crew believed it. Nobody blames them, though; it was such an easy lie to believe. He got the role of Jason Loane, a nineteen-year-old Hawaiian from Texas. Jason has the unique talent of getting on everyone's nerves.

Question to Ponder: Do you think Jason made a good decision by lying to get his job?

He is one of the main characters in the tenth season of *Baywatch*, which also doubled as the first season of *Baywatch Hawaii*. In this season, Mitch Buchannon, while dealing with the loss of his mother in Oahu, Hawaii, decides that he is going to establish an international team of lifeguards that includes new characters such as Kekoa Tanaka, Jason Ioane, Sean Monroe, Dawn

Masterton, Jessie Owens, J.D. Darius, and Allie Reese. Mitch puts Sean Monroe in charge of the lifeguards. Jason was on the series till 2001. He starred in forty-four episodes.

After the *Baywatch* series, Jason realized that he wanted to be an actor. At that time, he was enrolled to study marine biology at the University of Iowa. He left and traveled the world for a while. Then he moved to Los Angeles to actively pursue an acting career. At this point, Jason found it hard to get a manager for a while.

"Jason Momoa, Aquaman" by Eva Rinaldi Celebrity Photographer is licensed under CC BY-SA 2.0.

The Early 2000s

After the *Baywatch* series, he was in the chaotic sequel, "Baywatch: a Hawaiian Wedding" as Jason Loane again. Here, it is discovered that Mitch Buchannon didn't die as portrayed in the last episode of the tenth season. Instead, he is in Los Angeles recovering from amnesia. He has a new fiancée, Allison Ford, who strangely looks like his ex, who died in the seventh season of *Baywatch*. Taylor, who runs the Baywatch headquarters, now lures Mitch back so that he could introduce his fiancée to the members of Baywatch. Mitch's ex-girlfriend Neely is back. She wants to get back together with Mitch. She meets his fiancée and is suspicious of the resemblance between Allison and Stephanie.

C.J, who is launching a bar in Hawaii, invites the old members of Baywatch for the opening, including Caroline Holden, who is now an actress. He also asks John D. Cort and Eddie Kramer, who is now dating Caroline after ending things with his ex, Shauni. The reunion also features Lani McKenzie, now turned Hula Dancer, and is one of C.J's good friends. Also, Jason Loane and Kekoa Tanaka are now dating. They are also around for the reunion at C.J's bar.

Mitch calls C.J, telling him about his (Mitch's) engagement to Allison and telling him that they planned that the wedding will take place in Hawaii. Mason Sato, Mitch's old nemesis, also comes to the party. He is there to plot his revenge against Mitch. Sato takes pictures of Mitch's loved ones in order to plot his revenge against him.

Neely is still very wary of Allison, so she gets her fingerprints and gives them to Jason. Neely tells him to give his brother, who is a detective.

After the engagement party, they go to Haiku Island, the venue for the wedding. There, Sato's men capture Cort, Caroline, Summer, Lani, Hobie, and Eddie and proceed to drown them. They record it all on video. Jason and Kenkoa tell Neely that Allison is a criminal named Judy Radin, who was imprisoned for assault with a major weapon and forgery. Neely informs Mitch, who does not believe her. He confronts Allison; she confesses, telling him that Sato is her partner. Sato shows Mitch the video of his friends drowning.

Mitch and Neely save the friends, and Sato attacks again. The fight between Sato and Mitch ends when the boat's propeller kills Sato. Allison and Sato's men are arrested. Mitch calls off the wedding and reconciles with Neely. J.D. and Kekoa start a relationship again, same with Jason and Leigh. C.J. marries one of her co-workers, so there's an actual wedding.

Jason admitted that with only *Baywatch* on his resume, it was difficult to get an acting job. He cemented the acting lie.

Jason has refused to let his children see *Baywatch*. According to him, *Baywatch* never happened. They don't say the B-word at home.

In 2003, he was cast as Kala, Lily's nephew, in *Tempted*. The film's plot features Emma Burke, a woman who is having problems in different areas of her life, including in her marriage, with her kids, and her job as a paralegal. Then she gets the devastating phone call that Lily, the woman who raised her, is dead. Lily's dying wish is that Emma return her ashes to Hawaii. Emma decides to go even though her husband doesn't want her to. She goes to Hawaii and meets Lily's nephew, Kala; he is younger than she is. However, she falls for him. She begins an ill-fated extra-marital affair with Kala.

In Hawaii, Emma discovers more about her life. She finds out that her biological mother is alive and doesn't want to meet her. Her husband Mike flies in with their children, and Emma is forced to realize that what she has may not be what she desires. She has to make a tough decision, whether to leave the young man who adores her or return to a family where she is not appreciated. She chooses her family.

Jason Momoa's presence dominates the entire film. His character is likable. The film was criticized, especially the character of Emma Burke. Critics said that the script was terrible for really talented actors.

Jason Momoa got his big-screen debut in 2004, *The Johnson Family Vacation*. He played the role of Navarro. In one of the scenes, the Johnsons make a stop at what they think is a native American reservation, which is a casino. They go in and ask where they can see real old-school Indians. They are directed to Jason Momoa's character, who changes from his casino uniform to a stereotypical Native American attire.

In 2004, he was also part of the cast of the television series *North Shore*. He had a leading role. The series centers on the guests and members of staff of Grand Waimea Hotel and Resort located on the Northshore of Oahu, Hawaii. Jason played the role of Frankie Seau, the bartender of the hotel. At the end of the series, he is in a relationship with Tessa Lewis, a con artist who fraudulently finds her way to the assistant concierge position in the hotel.

After *North Shore*, In 2005, Jason also got another leading role in *Stargate Atlantis*.

The series follows the adventure of John Shepard and his military team from the earth. They explore the planets in the Pegasus galaxy using a device known as "stargate." This device was built centuries ago by an advanced race of humans known as the "Ancients" in the lost city of Atlantis, the planet of Lantea. The town was built up to ten million years ago, but the ancients were forced to leave their home due to plagues in the Milky Way galaxy. They move to the Pegasus galaxy, where they encounter the enemy known as Wraith. After years of war against Wraith, the ancients lost and had to sink their city under the Lantea's ocean, which is the Stargate.

Jason Momoa played the role of Ronon Dex, a military specialist. Ronon is from the planet Sateda. Wraith hunted his planet, so Ronon fled. He spent seven years running from the wraith. However, the wraith had already inserted a tracker in Ronon's neck. Ronon is introduced in season two. He meets Shepard and the tram; they help him get rid of the tracker. Then he joins the team as the fourth member replacing Lt. Ford.

When it was first released, the response to *Stargate Atlantis* was mediocre. Critics said it had more to offer. However, when it was released on DVD, it had better reviews. Critics mentioned that the series is highly recommended and should be treasured. The show has been nominated for 62 awards, including Emmys, and it won nineteen.

In 2005, while in a jazz club with friends, Jason met his childhood crush, Lisa Bonet. Jason mentioned that he and Lisa were at the right place at the right time. After Lisa introduced herself, Jason turned to his friend and pretended to scream; he was filled with fireworks.

Question to Ponder: How would you feel if your crush finally noticed you?

He even dreaded his hair to impress her. When they were done at the Jazz club, Jason asked Lisa for a ride back to his hotel. They stopped at Cafe 101 and drank Guinness while eating grits. Lisa revealed that they had been together since the day they met. While the attraction was not full-on, they liked each other, and Jason stayed.

While they met in 2005, their relationship did not get serious until he broke up with his longtime girlfriend, Simone Mckinick.

In 2007, he starred in the motion picture *pipeline*. The plot follows the story of six friends who surf the Banzai Pipeline, but only five return. Four years after the incident, even though the friends are determined to forget about the incident, they can't. Jason played the role of Kai, one of their friends.

In 2007, Jason and his girlfriend welcomed their first child together, a daughter named Lola. She is Jason's first child and Lisa's second.

Question to Ponder: How do you think Jason felt about having a baby?

Later in December 2008, The couple welcomed their second child together, a boy they named Nakoa-Wolf Manakauapo Namakaeha. His name Nakoa means warrior; Lisa admitted that he was given that name because he was born on a stormy night.

In 2008, Jason had an altercation with a man at a bar; the man injured Jason with a broken beer glass. Jason had to get surgery. He had a hundred and forty stitches on his eyebrow. While he recovered from surgery, the scar remains.

In 2009, Jason Momoa joined the cast of *The Game*, which was in its third season. He appeared in four episodes. He played the role of Roman, the love interest of Kelly Pitts, the ex-wife of NFL champion Jason Pitts. Roman is buff and athletic, but he lacks common sense. Roman's relationship with Kelly started as a fling. However, it progressed to an actual relationship when Kelly became sad about Roman moving on with another woman. However, their relationship goes south because of Roman's short temper. In one scene, Roman gets angry, frightening Kelly and her daughter Brittany. Luckily, Jason steps in and saves the day. Kelly ended things with Roman after that incident.

In 2010, he played the role of Mikey in the short film "Brown Bag Diaries: Ridin' the Blinds in B Minor." He was also the director and screenwriter.

In 2011, he was cast as Conan in *Conan the Barbarian*. The film is another interpretation of the Conan myth. The plot follows the story of Conan. Conan is Corin's son; Corin is the chief of barbarians. He goes through several challenges to become a warrior, killing his enemies on the way and returning home with the heads of his enemies; his father says he is a competent warrior but a violent one who is not prepared to use a sword. Corin's village is attacked by Zym, who wants to put together the pieces to the Acheron's mask to resurrect his wife and subjugate Hyboria. The parts of the mask are scattered all around the Barbarian countries. Zym gets the part of the mask in Conan's town and destroys everything, leaving Conan as the sole survivor. Conan swears vengeance.

Years after Corin's Barbarian town was destroyed, Conan becones a pirate. While traveling, he comes across a slave province and liberates them. He also meets a thief, El-Shan; Zym's guards were pursuing El-Shan. Conan lets himself get imprisoned with El-Shan. He escapes from prison and discovers that Zym is searching for a girl who is a pure-blood direct offspring of Acheron's sorcerers. He wants to sacrifice her and use her blood to release the mask's power.

Conan intercepts Zym and Marique, his daughter, while they try to kidnap Tamara, the descendant of Acheron sorcerers. He saves her from capture while pretending that he wants to exchange her for gold. However, Zym is attacked by Conan, who is stopped by Marique, who makes sand soldiers and poisons Conan with a sword. Conan is rescued by Tamara. They go back to Conan's ship; Artus, Conan's friend, nurses him to recovery. Zym's men attack the boat, killing several of Conan's men. However, Conan's men defeat them. Conan tells Artus to retreat with Tamara to Messantia. Conan goes to challenge Zym in his palace. One day, as Tamara returns to Conan's boat, Marique and Zym's men abduct her.

Conan discovers that Tamara has been captured; he goes to Argalon, asking Ela-Shan for help. He asks Elshan for assistance in entering Zym's palace. Zym plans to take Tamara's blood. He mends the mask. He also plans to use Tamara's body as a mortal vessel for his wife's soul.

Conan infiltrates Zym's followers; he confronts the monster guarding the dungeons. Conan disguises himself as one of Zym's followers, by killing a guard and stealing his robe. Now part of Zym's guards, Conan watches Zym put on Acheron's mask. Conan frees Tamara; she runs off as he fights with Zym. He recovers the sword that Marique stole from Corin, his father. As Tamara escapes, she is attacked by Marique, Conan hears her voice and comes to her rescue by slashing Marique's hand. Baroque is shoved inside a pit; something pierces her there.

Zym vows that he will take revenge on Conan. Escaping from Zym, Tamara and Conan are trapped on a bridge, and Zym attacks them. Zym uses the mask to resurrect the soul of his dead wife, Maliva, who was a powerful sorceress. As she is resurrected, Maliva's spirit starts to occupy Tamara. She begs Conan to allow her to fall; instead, Conan demolishes the bridge and jumps with Tamara. Zym drops into the lava crying out for his wife.

Conan accompanies Tamara to her place of birth, letting her know he will meet her in the future. Conan returns to his father's village and informs his father's memory that he has exacted vengeance against Zym, recovered the sword that was stolen from him, and restored Corin's honor.

The film made a box office total of $48,795,021. It was a box office failure when compared to its budget of $90 million. It received a lot of negative reviews on Rotten Tomatoes. It was criticized because of its excessive use of 3D animations. This was a disappointment to Jason because he had worked hard for the role. First, he had to bulk up ten kilos of muscle mass to fit into the role. Also, he told his friend that his portrayal of Conan would be convincing with a broken nose, so his friend should hit him. His friend punched him, giving him a broken nose— the pain.

Question to Ponder: How do you think Jason felt after the box office disappointment?

Before Jason Momoa was Famous

http://allaboutbookseries.com/JasonMomoaBeforeFamous

"Jason Momoa at Bluesfest" by badjonni is licensed under CC BY-NC-SA 2.0.

The Khal Drogo Era.

After So many roles, Jason landed the role of Khal Drogo in the HBO series *Game of Thrones*. To get this role, Jason performed the Haka—a traditional war dance from New Zealand.

It was a recurring role till his character was killed off. The part made him more popular than any of his previous roles. Khal Drogo, in the series, is a powerful warlord of the Dothraki people who has never been defeated in battle. To gain an alliance with Drogo, Viserys Targaryen marries his sister Daenerys. Drogo stops supporting Viserys when he talks about up to Westeros. Drogo kills Viserys when he threatens to kill Daenerys and their unborn child. Drogo goes to battle and comes back wounded. The wound leads to blood poisoning. Desperate, his wife, Daenerys, tells a servant girl to perform a spell on him, which leads to the death of their unborn child. Unfortunately, he is left in a catatonic state, barely able to speak or move. Daenerys kills him, using his funeral pyre to awaken her dragons. The series was critically acclaimed and was nominated for 32 Emmys in its eight seasons.

In 2013, *Game of Thrones* was listed by the Writers Guild of America as the 40th best-written series in television history. In 2015, *The Hollywood Reporter* ranked the show number four on their list of best TV shows, while in 2016, the series was placed seventh on Empire's list of "The 50 best TV shows ever." The same year, *Rolling Stone* named the show the twelfth "greatest TV Show of all time."

Question to Ponder: How do you think Jason felt to be part of such a big show?

After filming his role in *Game of Thrones*, Jason mentioned that he found it challenging to get new work. According to him, *Game of Thrones* had not aired, and he had not gained popularity at that time. He could not get any significant role. He and his family were starving. He said, "It's very challenging when you have babies and are completely in debt." Luckily when the series aired, he could charm viewers with his character. Even with that, he gained respect for the role, not more work. People loved Khal Drogo, but he couldn't even speak English.

Question to Ponder: Do you believe Jason's lack of work affected him?

In 2012, he got a role in a film that was a box office bomb. He played the role of Keegan, an assassin in *Bullet to the Head*. He starred alongside Sylvester Stallone in the film. The plot follows the assassination of a cop in New Orleans. Keegan was hired to kill the assassins who killed the cop. He killed one, leaving the other one, Bobo, alive. His employer, Morel, orders him, Keegan, to get an incriminating file from the local mob. He kills the mobster and gets the file. While all this is going on, there's a new detective who has come to investigate the death of the cop. The detective, Kwon, teams with Bobo, and they discover that Keegan is an ex-mercenary whom Morel has hired as an enforcer. Keegan traces one of Morel's workers to Bobo's house. Bobo and Kwon escape, leaving a bomb to detonate, which kills Keegan's men. Furious, Keegan swears revenge.

Keegan confronts Bobo when he comes to trade a file for a girl. Keegan kills Morel and then fights with Bobo. Bobo stabs Keegan's throat while Kwon shoots Keegan dead. The film was heavily criticized. In fact, Sylvester Stallone was nominated for the Razzie award for best actor.

After *Bullet to the Head*, Jason starred in *Road to Paloma*, for which he as a co-writer. In October 2011, Jason mentioned that he was writing, directing, and acting on his upcoming project. In February 2012, he started filming *Road to Paloma*. The plot of the film follows Wolf, who murdered his mother's rapist, then runs from the law. While on the run, he meets a drifter named Cash. He heads north to his sister's home, where he plans to spread his mother's ashes. Unfortunately, while still running from the law, spreading his mother's ashes might be more challenging than he bargained for. The film also featured Lisa Bonet. It was released in 2014 at the Sarasota Film Festival. It had a box office total of $937,000 against the budget of $600,000. It got good to average reviews from critics.

In 2014, Jason also was cast in *Debug*, a horror film. This was a new genre for Jason in a way. It was different from most of the other films he had acted in. Jason played the role of Iam, the ship's psychopathic AI. The film follows six computer programmers tasked with debugging the AI of an interstellar spaceship. Their mission is to reboot the spaceship floating randomly in space. It seems like an easy task, except that the AI finds new ways to kill them all.

Once they are aboard the spacecraft, each hacker is appointed to execute a task that will reboot the system. As they prepare to begin the assignment, Mel insists that he should be the head of the project because during their previous work release, Kaida, the lead programmer, had a fellow prisoner killed. Capra, the corrections officer, puts Mel in charge and they begin the mission. Once Capra restores power to the spacecraft, the prisoners get to work, each off on separate computer terminals and at different ship levels, communicating through virtual headsets.

The system enters into lockdown, trapping everyone on the vessel. With nothing to do, Capra chooses to explore the spacecraft. He finds a medical bay. Bored, Capra decides to try a medical procedure for fun. Capra straps himself to an arm vessel that would test his blood pressure. His arm is trapped and a needle appears with the AI system taking form in front of him. Capra is then injected with a kind of nanotechnology that turns him into an assassin for the AI.

Kaida and James work together and start to encounter the illusions caused by the AI. Meanwhile, the AI system tricks Mel and Lara, secret lovers, and lures them into trouble. The AI starts to use fears and interests to go after them. Samson, one of the hackers, is scared of rats, so he sets a trap for the rat, and the AI system traps him using the trap he set for the rat. Diondra, another hacker, links into the AI system to reboot it. The mischievous AI program tempts her with a cube that is full of bank accounts from the former crew that boarded the spacecraft. The members of that crew all went missing. Following the cube, Diondra is led to a sewage pipe; she sees a decayed dead body and kicks the body down the pipe. After kicking it, she discovers that the dead body has a cube on it. Diondra desperately follows the body to find the cube; the AI system locks the door behind her, flooding the pipe with sewage.

James, Mel, and Kaida convene after experiencing all the weird things the AI system is doing. Mel and Kaida get into an argument; James defends her; then Capra comes and attacks the hackers. Kaida kills Capra by closing down the airlock on him.

James is wounded and becomes unconscious, and Kaida enters into the AI system simulation. There, she goes face to face with the main AI system and fights with it. Eventually, she dismantles the AI, but she is stuck inside the AI system. James wakes up and is now one of the only survivors with Kaida.

The movie ends by showing James, who is now the captain of the same spacecraft, and Kaida who currently exists in the virtual world as the AI operating system. The duo leads a new expedition with a new crew. The film was highly criticized. It got a lot of bad ratings and reviews.

Jason also acted in *Wolves*. The film follows Cayden, a high school football star who becomes a drifter after killing his parents when he turns into a werewolf. He meets Joe, a werewolf who explains more about werewolves, classifying them into purebloods and the bitten. He tells him that they are both purebloods and if he wants to learn more about them he should go to Lupin Ridge. He travels to Lupin Ridge, where he is hired as a farmhand. He meets his cousin who warns him to leave the town. His cousin is killed and eaten by Connor (Jason Momoa's character) and his pack.

Cayden learns that the alpha, Connor, is his father. Cayden goes to Connor to reveal himself, but Connor unleashes his pack on Cayden. Overwhelmed, Cayden escapes, then starts to find a way to defeat Connor. Cayden defeats Connor, and Connor reveals that he was in love with Cayden's mother. Wild Joe comes, revealing that he planned everything all along, from the murder of Cayden's adoptive parents to his return because he wanted Cayden to kill Connor. Joe kills Connor while Cayden kills Joe.

The film was heavily criticized. Critics described the plot as lazy.

In 2014, he was also in the series *The Redline*. He played the role of Philip Kopus, a dangerous, charismatic man filled with self-confidence. He is part of the Lenape tribe and an ex-convict. His return to the tribe is suspicious as they all seem to think that his arrival may threaten the peace especially when He got into conflict with Police Officer Jensen. The series was well-received as it received a lot of positive reviews from critics.

Jason also appeared in two episodes of *Drunk TV*.

"Jason Momoa" by Gage Skidmore is licensed under CC BY-SA 2.0.

Aquaman Era

Everybody loved Jason as Khal Drogo, including Zack Snyder and his wife, Deborah. The DC producers loved the idea of Jason Momoa as Aquaman because of his performance as Drogo. After Zack and Deborah watched *Game of Thrones*, Zack told Deborah that Jason would be a good fit as Aquaman. According to them, he was, though, and he had the vibe that came from the water. When it was time for the Aquaman auditions, Zack invited Jason for the auditions. At first, he didn't want to go; he was invited for a general audition for *Batman*, and he knew he was not going to be Batman. However, his manager called and pushed him to go, informing him that Zack Snyder wanted to see him. So, Jason went anyway. He did the opposite of what Batman was. He pretended Batman died and he picked his suit from the alleyway and did his thing.

After his audition, Zack called him in. Zack asked him if he knew why he was called and Jason replied that he didn't. At that point, Ben Affleck had been cast as Batman. Then Zack revealed that he wanted Jason to play Aquaman. Jason was very excited. Even though he didn't finish his degree in marine biology, Jason is still a friend to the sea creatures and he makes the perfect king of the seven seas.

Question to Ponder: How do you think Jason felt after he was asked to play Aquaman?

Jason had his Aquaman debut in 2016, *Batman vs. Superman: Dawn of Justice*, where he made a cameo appearance. He was underwater, wielding his trident in footage in the computer file stolen from Lex Luthor.

He also starred in Netflix's *Frontier* as the main character Declan Harp. He is an Irish American leading campaigns to end the monopoly of Hudson Bay Company on the sale of furs in Canada. The company is corrupt and also involved in illegal trade. The series recevied mixed reviews from critics. The storytelling in the series was described as sluggish. However, critics praised Jason Momoa's acting in the series. The series was nominated for a total of ten Canadian Screen Awards in 2017 and 2018, including Best Achievement in Casting, Best Direction in a Dramatic Series, Best Costume Design, and Best Performance by an Actor in a Continuing Leading Dramatic Role, for which Jason Momoa was nominated. It won the Best Achievement in Make-Up Award. It was also nominated for three Directors Guild of Canada Awards.

http://allaboutbookseries.com/JasonFrontier

Jason also acted in *Once upon a Time in Venice*. He played the role of Spyder, a drug lord, who kidnapped the dog of Steve Ford, the main character. Spyder forces Steve to engage in different tasks for his dog's safety. One of the tasks involves drugs. The film was released for a limited period. It was highly criticized.

He also played the role of Joe Bright in *Sugar Mountain*.

In 2017, Jason Momoa got into his superhero role. Just before he emerged himself in the DC superhero role of Aquaman, Jason played the role of Miami man in *The Bad Batch*. The film's plot follows a young woman Arlen, who is exiled to a desert where people undesired by society live. These people are known as "the bad batch." These people are outside the USA and free from US laws. Arlen is abducted by two women, one of whom cuts her right arm and leg. She tricks the woman into unchaining her, kills the woman, and escapes. A mute hermit rescues her and takes her to Comfort, a nightclub where she is taken care of.

Five months later, Arlen has healed; she's sporting a prosthetic leg now. She patrols the desert frequently. It is in one of these patrols that she sees a woman and a girl scavenging a golf cart. She accuses the woman of being a cannibal and kills her. She takes the girl to the hermit, who checks on her.

She takes hallucinogens, which causes her to lose the young girl. Subsequently, she goes on another patrol where she meets "Miami Man." He is the leader of the cannibals, and he's in search of his daughter, the young girl who was with Arlen previously. He threatens to kill her; then she reveals where his daughter is.

As they journey back to Comfort, Arlen and the Miami Man grow closer. In their journey, Miami Man kills a cannibal who was going to trade Arlen's blood for gas. The Miami man gets shot and Arlen has to return to Comfort alone. She goes to find the young girl who has been living with Dream, the leader of the comfort. After threatening one of his pregnant concubines with a gun, she gets the girl and escapes. They reunite with Miami Man, and Arlen lets him know that she wants to be in the desert with him. He tells her that the desert is not a place for her, but he doesn't send her away. The film ends with the trio eating the young girl's rabbit.

After this film, Jason immersed himself in his Aquaman title. He joined the Justice League as Aquaman and he wowed us with his role. The plot stems a thousand years back when Steppenwolf and his league of parademons tried to take control of the earth using the joint energies of the three Mother Boxes. Fortunately, the operation was stopped by an alliance that contained the Olympian Gods, Atlanteans, Amazons, humans, and extra-terrestrial beings. After Steppenwolf's army is destroyed, the Mother Boxes are separated and concealed.

In the present, Superman has died two years earlier and his death triggered the reactivation of the Mother Boxes and subsequently Steppenwolf's return to Earth. Steppenwolf plans to gather the boxes to establish "The Unity," which will destroy Earth and revamp it to look like Steppenwolf's homeworld.

Steppenwolf takes a Mother Box from Themyscira, causing Queen Hippolyta to warn Diana, her daughter. Diana informs Bruce Wayne, and together, they plan to unite other superheroes to their aim. Aquaman refuses to join the league but when an Atlantean outpost is attacked to retrieve another Mother Box, Arthur Curry/Aquaman decides to join. The team is composed of Bruce Wayne, Diana, Barry Allen, Arthur Curry, and Victor Stone. Victor Stone helps them get the next box. Bruce Wayne decides that they use it to resurrect Superman after Victor Stone informs them that the box was used to reconstruct his body. They resurrect Superman, but he does not remember anything, so he attacks them. They invite Lois Lane, who takes him back to Smallville where he regains his memory. In the midst of the chaos, the Mother Box is left unguarded and Steppenwolf steals the box. The superheroes go to a small village to attempt to stop Steppenwolf from joining the boxes. Superman arrives and assists them in defeating Steppenwolf, whose parademons are fighting against him. After the battle, Bruce and Diana set up a base for the team creating space for new members.

The film was a box office bomb. It also got a lot of negative critical responses. Fans were surprised at the direction the film took. Zack Snyder has to leave during filming to mourn the death of his daughter. The new director did a lot of refilming, changing the themes and contradicting some of the characters when compared to their individual films. The director of Wonder Woman, Patty Jenkins openly expressed her dislike for the film. She mentioned that the character of Wonder Woman was different when compared to Wonder Woman films. Also, many fans complained about it and advocated for Zack Snyder's cut of Justice League. The actors of the film also spoke about Snyder's cut. Jason Momoa spoke about Snyder's cut revealing that Snyder's cut was to introduce the Aquaman film. In an interview during the Aquaman tour, Jason was asked about the place of Aquaman within the more considerable continuity of the DCEU. He replied that the film took place after Justice League, Zack's cut. He mentioned that the ending showed that Arthur Curry was warned of an upcoming conflict by Mera and Vulko. Arthur refuses their request for assistance, informing them that he was going home to see his father.

After this interview, Zack Snyder released that snippet of his director's cut. For fans, it was further proof that Zack Snyder's director's cut existed so they began to push for it to be released. Jason Momoa was very vocal about wanting the cut to be released.

The film was shortlisted as a potential nominee for best visuals for the 90th Academy Awards, but it didn't make it to the nomination list. However, it won the Golden Schmoes Awards for Biggest Disappointment. It also won second place in the Oklahoma Film Critics Circle Awards "Most Disappointing Film."

2018 came with more roles for Jason Momoa. He was the protagonist, Joe Braven in *Braven*. The film's plot follows Joe Braven, the owner of a logging company, who lives with his wife and daughter, Stephanie and Charlotte. Joe's father Lindon, who suffers from brain trauma, gets into a bar brawl. Stephanie advises her husband to spend time with his father at the family cabin on a secluded mountain. Joe agrees and goes to the mountain with his father. Meanwhile, Charlotte was hiding at the back of the car so she could tag along.

A drug trafficker asks Joe's coworker Weston to recruit drivers to help transport drugs. Weston refuses. The duo gets into an accident, displacing the log of woods and cocaine. Weston suggests that they keep the drugs in Joe's cabin.

Joe discovers the cocaine in a shed after they get to the cabin. He manages to hide Charlotte just before the cabin gets surrounded by Kassen, the drug lord, and his men. Unable to call for help, Joe arms himself with a bow and arrow and Linden a gun. Weston attempts to act as an intermediary, but Kassen kills him.

Joe drives out with Charlotte to get a cellular network. Joe tells Charlotte to climb the mountain and call her mom. Charlotte follows his instruction; she calls her mom, who calls the sheriff. Kassen finds the bag but it's empty. He finds out where Joe sent Charlotte and sends one of his men to get her. Stephanie gets to the mountain just in time to stop Kassen's mercenary from getting Charlotte. Charlotte is picked up by the sheriff. Kassen takes Linden hostage and, after Joe pleads for his father's life, Kassen kills Linden. Kassen also shoots the sheriff and escapes from the cabin; he retrieves the lost cocaine. Joe chases after him and runs into Stephanie and helps her kill the mercenary trying to kill her. Joe finds Kassen and pushes Jim off a cliff, killing him, before being reunited with Stephanie and Charlotte. The film earned positive reviews, and its aggregate ratings are favorable.

After *Braven*, we got to see a film dedicated to Aquaman. The film gave an in-depth view of Arthur Curry's character. The plot follows the sequel of Zack Snyder's Justice League. The film begins in Maine in 1985, where Thomas Curry, a lighthouse keeper, rescued Atlanna, the Queen of Atlantis, in the course of a storm. Thomas and Atlanna fall in love and give birth to a son, Arthur. As a young child, Arthur could talk with sea creatures. Atlanna is forced to leave her family when King Orvax, the ruler of Atlantis sent Atlantean soldiers to fetch Atlanna, who had escaped from her arranged marriage in Atlantis. After defeating them, Atlanna leaves her family, promising to return when it's safe. In Atlantis, she charges her adviser, Nuidis Vulko, to teach Arthur. Arthur grows older and despises Atlantis once he learns that Orvax executed Atlanna for loving a human and having a "half-breed" son.

The present begins a year after Steppenwolf's defeat. In a fight with pirates, Arthur killed the leader who was trying to kill him. David, The son of the leader vows to take revenge. In Atlantis, Marius, Arthur's younger brother, wants to unite the underwater kingdoms and then destroy the earth's surface because humans have been polluting the seas. He asks Nereus, the king of Xebel, who agrees to join him. Meera, Nereus' daughter, refuses to join. Instead, she goes to the surface to ask Arthur for help. Arthur returns to Atlantis with Meera. Vulko tells him to get the Atlan's trident so he can claim his place on the throne.

Arthur and Meera begin their journey. They travel to the desert where they uncover a holographic message. The message guides them to Sicily, where they get the trident's coordinates.

Marius imprisons Nuidis Vulko and pressures the Fishermen Kingdom to pledge their allegiance to him by killing their king and coercing the queen and princess to accept the allegiance. He also gives David a prototype Atlantean battle suit to kill Arthur; It is also indicated that Marius hired David and his father to hijack the Russian submarine that attacked Atlantis earlier, to win Nereus's backing. David now calls himself Black Manta. He injures Arthur during a fight in Italy, but Arthur defeats him.

Following the coordinates, Arthur and Meera get to their destination. There, Arthur and Mera fight the Trench monsters. They are transported by a wormhole to an unexplored part of the sea at the center of the Earth. They meet Atlanna, who had been living in the uncharted sea for twenty years after she was sacrificed to the Trench for Arthur's illegitimate birth. She survived the trenches, and escaped to the uncharted sea, alive and well.

Arthur faces the Karathen, keeper of the trident, who is a mythical leviathan. Arthur voices his determination to protect Atlantis and the surface; he reclaims the trident and gains control over the seven seas.

Marius leads his army against the Brine Kingdom to declare himself Ocean Master, while Arthur, with Mera, Karathen, and the Trench, leads their army of marine animals against Marius. Marius' followers accept Arthur as the true king once they learn that he holds Atlan's trident. Marius is defeated by Arthur but Arthur spares his life, and Marius is imprisoned. Marius accepts the imprisonment once he discovers that Arthur rescued their mother. Atlanna reunites with Thomas as promised, and Arthur is crowned King.

The film was widely accepted. It got a total box office gross of $1.148 billion making it the highest-grossing DC installment and highest-grossing film based on a DC character. It is also Warner Brothers' second-highest-grossing film worldwide behind *Harry Potter and the Deathly Hallows – Part 2* ($1.342 billion). It was the fifth most profitable film of 2018, with a net profit of $260.5 million. The film received a lot of positive reviews. Fans and critics generally praised Jason Momoa's acting skills. The film was nominated for several awards. Jason Momoa was nominated for two kids' choice awards: favorite actor and favorite superhero for his performance in the movie. He was also nominated for the MTV Movie and TV award for Best Kiss with Amber Heard. He was also nominated for teen choice awards as a choice sci-fi/fantasy movie actor. Jason mentioned that his experience growing up as a mixed kid helped him understand Arthur Curry's experience in Aquaman. He also mentioned that performing stunts underwater was difficult. As

Aquaman, he did all his stunts in justice league, but the stunts in the Aquaman film were many.

He was also injured.

In the wake of the *Aquaman* premiere, Jason Momoa hosted Saturday Night Live. He pulled off the sketches. The Christmas episode of the elf on the shelf was hilarious. When Jason played the role of Khal Drogo in Game of Thrones, we were wowed. In this episode of SNL, Jason played the role of Khal Drogo in the sketch titled "Khal Drogo's Ghost Dojo. The sketch is a talk show that features dead people from the *Game of Thrones* series. The final sketch, "First impression," is about a Christmas dinner. There Jason Momoa plays a middle-aged father who is having a Christmas dinner with his daughter and her fiancé. The fiancé, played by Beck Beckett, decides it is a good time to play hide and seek. It was hilarious. We also see him in the sleigh ride with Cecily Strong and the "Day of the Dorks" sketch. Jason showed us that he can be effortlessly funny and he's not the brooding macho guy all the time. The fake commercials were also hilarious. He described hosting SNL as a dream come true.

In 2019, Jason Reprised his role as Aquaman in the Warner Brothers' film *The Lego Movie 2: The Second Part*. He acted as the voice of Aquaman.

In October 2019, Jason starred in the third episode of the *Simpsons*, season thirty-one. Jason played the role of Jason Momoa in the episode. At a Carnival in San Castellaneta, Mayor Quimby introduced Jason Momoa as Aquaman himself. There are a lot of cheers from the crowd. Jason gives a speech and then people in the carnival discover that they've been pickpocketed. Jason dives into the water. The episode was fun to watch; I mean, it's the Simpsons. It was rated four of five stars.

Later in 2019, Jason was in the Apple TV series "See" as one of the leading characters. He plays the role of Baba Voss, the fearless leader of the Alkenny Tribe. He's the husband of Maghra, the older brother of Edo Voss, and the adopted father of Kofun and Haniwa. The plot of the film is set in the twenty-first century after a deadly virus has hindered humans of their sight. In this era, people with vision are rare and when they are seen they are hunted by the witchfinders.

A pregnant Maghra seeks shelter with the Alkenny tribe. It's revealed that the biological father of her children, Jerlamarel, has his vision. Word spreads that he has children who can also see, so they are being hunted. It is left to Baba Voss to protect his tribe and family from the witchfinders. Since its release, the film has received mixed reviews from critics. Some find it interesting, but some others have described it as a waste of Jason Momoa's talent. However, the series has been nominated for some awards, including IGN's best action series of 2019, winning other prizes.

"Jason Momoa Aquaman, Sydney, Australia, 19th Dec, 2018" by humanstatuebodyart is licensed under CC BY-SA 2.0.

Jason Momoa in The New Decade

In 2020, Jason Momoa produced a documentary on how native Americans are trying to recover their foodways. It covers the efforts of native Americans in food sovereignty. The documentary studies the culinary and eating habits of native Americans, from Yurok men in Northern California, teaching their tribes' traditional practices for fishing and preparing salmon on the Klamath River. The documentary features the historical agricultural practices of the White Mountain Apache, San Carlos Apache, and Yavapai people. The documentary received positive reviews. Valerie Schloredt described it as *"wide-ranging, addressing both systemic issues and small-scale solutions"* in a *YES! Magazine* review. Marc Casanovas called it "the best documentary of the year in the United States." He also mentioned that the documentary is "a cry in favor of food sovereignty and recognizing the generational trauma" embedded in native American people. Apart from positive reviews, it also won the Best Documentary Feature at the Red Nation Film Festival Awards in 2020. *The New York Times* also called it a critic's pick.

In 2021, We finally saw Zack Snyder's cut of Justice League. The film is the follow-up film to *Batman vs. Superman: Dawn of Justice*. The ultimate edition of Justice League received lukewarm reviews. The new director, Joss Whedon rewrote a large part of the script. Snyder's cut got positive early reviews from critics. Most of the scenes in Snyder are new. First, we see that Ray Fisher's role as Cyborg has more screen time. Before the release of the 2016 version,

Snyder mentioned that Cyborg was the heart of this movie and he was. Cyborg's character is central to the plot of the film.

We have a backstory on Flash. Also, there's Darkseid, who is a boss to Steppenwolf. In this cut, Darkseid is the one who attacked earth first. Darkseid is defeated by the allied forces and is forced to withdraw from battle when Ares' battle-axe injures his shoulder. He sent Steppenwolf to unite the Mother Box to complete the work. In this version, the parademons don't smell fear. Let's not forget that there's a lot of blood. Snyder's cut has a different ending from the cinema version. The film was well-received. According to the content intelligence company, Snyder's cut had the fourth largest engagement on social media, just behind Squid Games, Wandavision, and Loki. It was the eighth most-streamed film of 2021 and the second most pirated film of 2021. Most of the critics agreed that it was superior when compared to the 2016 film. It received accolades from MTV Movie & TV Awards, Golden Trailer Awards, Critics Super Choice Awards, Clio Awards, and others. Jason Momoa was thrilled about the release of Snyder's cut. He talked about it a lot during his Aquaman tour. This made fans clamor for the release of the film.

Jason was also one of the producers of *Sweet Girl*, an action thriller he also acted in. He played the role of Ray Cooper. The plot explores the story of Amanda Cooper who has been diagnosed with a rare form of cancer. Unfortunately, days before she begins treatment, the drug is taken off the market due to Simon Keeley, the company Bioprime CEO, bribing the manufacturer to delay production. So, Ray calls Keeley, threatening him to reverse his decision or he will kill him. Keeley ignores this threat and Ananda dies, leaving behind Ray and their daughter Rachael.

Six months after the death of his wife, Ray gets a call about the illegal activity happening in Bioprime. The caller, Martin, has evidence about the activity. Unknown to Ray and Martin, they are followed by Rachel and Santos, a hitman. Martin tells Ray that BioPrime has been bribing anyone who questions their dirty deeds. Before he can share his evidence, Santos stabs him dead. As the train stops at a station, Santos stabs Ray and knocks out Rachel, leaving them both on the platform to die.

Two years after the train incident, Ray dresses as a waiter to enter Keeley's charity. He had been obsessively tracking Keeley for the past two years. After interrogating Keeley, he tells him to ask Vinod Shah, the company chairman. Convinced that her father has gone too far, Rachel contacts FBI Agent Sarah Meeker and tries to convince her to look into BioPrime. Ray decides to go after Shah. Rachel helps him trap Shah. Ray begins to interrogate him, but Shah refuses to talk and is killed by Santos. Ray and Rachel meet with Santos in a diner, and after Santos admits that he finds himself sympathetic to Ray's cause, he reveals that Congresswoman Diana Morgan is his real employer. He also tells Rachel that they will meet again soon.

Returning to the city, Ray is ambushed by the FBI and flees to the roof of PNC Park. As Meeker tries to talk him down, it's revealed that "Ray" is actually Rachel. Ray died from his wounds at the subway and Rachel, suffering from PTSD and dissociative identity disorder devoted herself to finishing his quest for vengeance. She jumps into the Allegheny River but gets knocked

unconscious and put in an ambulance. After breaking free and crashing the vehicle, she locates

Morgan's campaign office, where Santos is waiting. Despite his initially managing to subdue her

by strangling and drowning her, Rachel is able to regain her strength and stabs Santos to death.

She confronts Morgan and secretly records her admitting she was bribed by BioPrime for

government contracts and that she ordered the hit on Bennett and Ray. Rachel flees and sends

the recording to the FBI. In the aftermath, Morgan is arrested for her crimes, while Rachel obtains

a fake passport and travels.

After Sweet Girl in 2021, Jason played the role of Duncan Idaho in the Sci-Fi film *Dune: Part One*. Duncan is the swordmaster of House Atreides and one of Paul's mentors. Talking about *Dune*, Jason mentioned that when he first saw the *Dune* trailer, "It was 'Josh Brolin, Jason Momoa, Javier Bardem,' and he was just like, 'Oh my god. I can't believe my name was with those names.'"

The film was made after the sci-fi novel *Dune*. It is the second theatrical adaptation of the book. Fans hoped that the film would do justice to the book better than the 1984 film. After Paramount failed to produce a successful film, Legendary Entertainment bought the rights to make the film. They only have the rights to produce the first film. The approval of the second film depended on the first film's success.

Luckily, the first film was successful. As of March 2022, the film had a worldwide box office total of $400.7 million. It also did well when it was released on VOD services. *Dune* debuted at the second position on iTunes and Vudu charts and ranked seventh on Google Play. It was critically acclaimed. It got so many positive reviews right from its early premiere at the Venice Film Festival. It was praised for the writing and striving to be as original as the book. *Dune* was nominated for ten Academy Awards and it won six. It also got nominated for three Golden Globe Awards winning one. It gets better; it was nominated for eleven British Academy Film Awards and won five. It had ten nominations for the Critics' Choice Movie Awards and won three. It also had two AACTA International Awards nominations, winning one. It was nominated for ten Satellite Awards winning five, one Grammy Award, and one Hollywood Music in Media Awards, which it won. It was also nominated for four People's Choice Awards, one Nickelodeon Kids' Choice Award which it won, one Screen Actors Guild Award, and three Dorian Awards, winning one, among others. Most of the awards were for writing and technical achievements. *Dune* was named as one of the top 10 films of 2021.

Based on the success of the first film, the second film will be released in October 2023.

Jason Momoa Stars as Duncan Idaho

http://allaboutbookseries.com/JasonDuncanIdaho

In 2022, Jason Momoa appeared in an uncredited Cameo in DC's *Peacemaker* series.

"Jason Momoa speaking at the 2015 Phoenix Comicon at the Phoenix Convention Center in Phoenix, Arizona." by Gage Skidmore is licensed under the Creative Commons Attribution-Share Alike 2.0 Generic license.

Future Projects

Jason Momoa has future projects in his filmography. They include

Slumberland: This is an adventure movie based on the book *Little Nemo in Slumberland*. Netflix will distribute the film when it is released in 2022. Jason plays the role of Flip. In the film version, a young girl, Nemo works with an outlaw, Flip, to see her late father again in the dreamworld of Slumberland. The film is in post-production.

Jason is also working on the Sequel of *Aquaman*, *Aquaman and the Lost Kingdom*. Jason Momoa pitched the idea for the sequel during the production of the first film. James Wan, the director of the film, didn't want to rush a sequel. However, in January 2019, Wan agreed to supervise the sequel. In 2020, it was announced that Wan would be directing the film. Jason Momoa is also a co-writer. It is currently in post-production and will be released in 2023. The film follows after the first film where Black Manta was taken by a scientist Dr. Stephen Shin, who is obsessed with finding Atlantis.

As Jason is growing in DC's extended universe, he is also growing in Hollywood. The actor has joined the *Fast and Furious* franchise. He is going to play the role of a villain in *Fast X*. His character will be announced later. Filming started in April 2022 and Jason began filming his scenes in May. The actor would also be in the final film of the franchise.

Jason Momoa is also going to play the role of Big Jam in *The Last Manhunt*. The release date is still yet to be announced. He's also the executive producer of the film.

He's also going to play a role in the *Chief of War* series. His role and the movie release date are yet to be announced as it is still in development.

Jason Momoa's Awards and Lifetime Achievements

For his many roles, Jason has received worldwide attention, especially for his roles as Khal Drogo in the hit HBO max series, *Game of Thrones*, and the DC Comic character Aquaman in the movie *Aquaman*. His exceptional acting prowess has given him a notable reputation in the acting industry. In the course of his career, Jason has earned a total of seven nominations for various awards, of which he won one (1). `

All of Jason Momoa's Nominations for various awards are listed out below:

He was nominated for the Cinemacon Awards once as

- Male Rising Star (Conan the Barbarian and Game of Thrones) - 2011

He was nominated for the Scream Awards once for

- Best Ensemble (*Game of Thrones*) - 2011

He was nominated for Screen Guild Actors Awards for

- Outstanding performance by an ensemble in a drama series (*Game of Thrones*) - 2011

He was nominated for the Canadian Screen Awards for

- Best Actor in a Continuing Leading Dramatic Role (*Frontier*) - 2017

He was also nominated for the Nickelodeon Kids' Choice Awards twice for

- Favorite Movie Actor (*Aquaman*) - 2019

- Favorite Superhero (*Aquaman*) - 2019

He was also nominated for MTV Movie and TV Awards for

- Best Kiss (which was shared with Amber Heard) (*Aquaman*) - 2019

He was also nominated for the Teens Choice Awards once for

- Choice Sci-Fi/Fantasy Movie Actor (*Aquaman*) – 2019

Out of all these nominations, he won only one award. That is the Cinemacon Awards for

- Male Rising Star (Conan the Barbarian and Game of Thrones) - 2011

His Other Achievements

Jason's movie, *Aquaman*, is still the most popular of his movies since his career started. It made a total of $1.148 billion making it the highest-grossing DC installment and highest-grossing film based on a DC character. It is also Warner Brothers' second-highest-grossing film worldwide.

His other movie, *Game of Thrones*, where he plays the character Khal Drogo was also listed by the Writers Guild of America as the 40th best-written series in television history. It was also ranked number four by the Hollywood Reporter in their list of best TV shows and ranked seventh on Empire's list of best TV shows in 2016. The same year *Rolling Stone* named the show the twelfth "greatest TV Show of all time." His character also received a lot of positive reviews and compliments. Another feat Jason attained was the documentary that he produced. It won Best Documentary Feature at the Red Nation Film Festival Awards in 2020.

Jason has also shown his great love for partying and drinking. This is evident in the tattoo he has on his arm which is a French phrase that means "Always be drunk." He also expressed his favorite beer to be Guinness and luckily for him, Guinness decided to create a beer specifically for his character Khal Drogo from *Game of Thrones*. The beer is named "Mano Beer" and this is a big win for Jason as it is Guinness's first-ever sour beer. The beer bottle is designed with Hawaiian flowers and also has a motif that's similar to the tattoo on Jason's arm.

What's more is the fact that Jason Momoa has his own production company. He created the company in 2010, a year before *Game of Thrones* aired. The company is named Pride of Gypsies, and this is also his username on Instagram. When asked for the meaning behind the name, it was said that it referred to a pride of lions while Gypsy was used to describe a person who was free-spirited. This company has produced quite a number of ads and also trailers for various movies. They've also produced movies in which Jason has starred. The company produced Road to *Paloma*, *Braven*, and even *Sweet Girl*.

While working in a surf shop, Jason was discovered by the renowned designer Takeo Kobayashi who urged him to enter into a modeling career. Luckily for Jason, he agreed and decided to give modeling a try. Just a year after, Jason was named Hawaiian Model of the Year. Jason Momoa is also said to be gifted in playing the guitar.

"1991 Steinberger Sceptre electric guitar" by tawalker is licensed under CC BY 2.0.

Jason Momoa's Charity and Advocacy Work

A lot of celebrities are known to either support charity events and foundations or even have their own personal charity foundations. Jason Momoa is no different. He is well known as a supporter of the charity organization, Sustainable Coastlines Hawaii. This organization is a local organization that is handled by a few individuals and backed up by voluntary supporters. It's a non-profit organization that encourages people in the local community to keep their coastlines clean by engaging in cleanups of the beach. The organization organizes educational programs, offers waste diversion services, and conducts campaigns in order to increase public awareness.

He also managed to raise money for Sustainable Coastlines Hawaii with the assistance of Ellen Degeneres's friends at Shutterfly. To win the money, he had to throw an axe at a target. Luckily, Jason was able to raise a total of $31,000 for the organization.

In 2016, Jason Momoa's picture was also published on the front cover of Wednesday's edition of *USA Today*. This was distributed in New York, Las Vegas, Washington, DC, Baltimore, Los Angeles, Chicago, and Detroit. In the publication, Jason spoke on water and sustainability, encouraging the reader and viewers to take the initiative of working to solve the issue of water and sustainability.

Also, Jason Momoa has expressed his position against the single-use of plastics in Hollywood. To support this position, he became a co-founder of Mananalu. Mananalu was set up to ensure sustainability in the entertainment industry while on set. Mananalu offers water packaged in cans that are aluminum and can be recycled continuously. Mananalu partnered with Earth Angel since they share the same objectives. The CEO and founder of Earth Angel, Emellie O'Brien commended Jason's act and interest in providing solutions for a sustainable environment. To create more awareness of the negative effect of single-use plastics, Jason shaved his long-grown beard in a video while addressing the issue. It doesn't stop here as he later went ahead to auction his beard trimmer, which was signed by him, on eBay. His intention was for the proceeds to go straight to the non-profit environmental charity, The Nature Conservancy.

His good work doesn't stop here. Jason Momoa has also volunteered with the Make A Wish Foundation in order to spend time with some of his young fans who are terminally ill. Also, Jason Momoa's lifestyle brand collaborated with So iLL and Snake Bite Co. in order to make face masks during the covid pandemic. The money received was for the purpose of charity.

Also, in 2020, Jason decided to participate in Fanatics All-In Challenge as a means to help fight against food insecurity. Michael Rubin, the founder of Fanatics, had started this challenge in order to help people in dire need, like the elderly ones, kids, and even frontline workers. This fundraising event encourages fans to engage in a rare opportunity experience with various celebrities while also donating money for the common good. The money received from this event is donated to charity organizations like Meals on Wheels, Feeding America, No Kid Hungry, and World Central Kitchen.

"Jason Momoa at the Florida Supercon in 2014" by steve cranston is licensed under the Creative Commons Attribution-Share Alike 2.0 Generic license.

Jason Momoa's Timeline

1979 - Jason Momoa was born on August 1, 1979, in Hawaii before moving to Iowa with his mom.

1998 - When he was 19, Jason got a job at a surf shop in Hawaii. He also auditioned for a role in the movie Baywatch Hawaii. Luckily he got the role of Jason Loane, a 19-year-old Hawaiian from Texas.

1997- Jason graduated high school.

1999 - He won the 1999 Hawaii's Model of the year.

2003 - Jason was in the *Baywatch* sequel, "A Hawaiian Wedding." He was also cast in the movie *Tempted* for the role of Kala, Lily's nephew.

2004 - He finally got his big-screen debut in the movie The Johnson Family Vacation. Jason was also cast in the television series North Shore for a leading role.

2005 - He got cast for a leading role in another television series, Stargate Atlantis. Here, Jason played the role of Ronon Dex who is a military specialist. He also met his crush, who is currently his wife, Lisa Bonet.

2007 - Jason starred in the motion picture movie, Pipeline, playing the role of Kai. He also welcomed his first child, a girl named Lola, along with his girlfriend Lisa.

2008 - Jason welcomed his second child with his girlfriend but this time around a boy. He was named Nakoa-Wolf because he was born on a stormy night. That same year, Jason got into a fight with a man at a bar and got injured with a broken beer glass. He had to receive a total of a hundred and forty stitches with surgery.

2009 - He joined the cast of The Game in its third season. He played the role of Roman, the love interest of Kelly Pitts, and appeared for just four episodes.

2010 - Jason is cast in the short movie *Brown Bag Diary: Ridin' the Blinds in B Minor* for the role of Mikey. Apparently, he directed the movie and also wrote the screenplay. Jason also founded a production company with his friend, Brian Andrew Mendoza.

2011 - Based on the Conan myth, Jason was cast to play the character of Conan in the movie *Conan the Barbarian*. He also got the role of Khal Drogo in the popular and hit HBO Series *Game of Thrones*. These two movies got him nominated for three different awards. The Cinemacon Awards, The Scream Awards, and the Screen Guild Actors Awards. Jason won the Cinemacon Awards for the category of Male Rising Star for both movies: *Conan the Barbarian* and *Game of Thrones*.

2012 - Jason finally got a role after *Game of Thrones*. He was cast as Keegan an assassin in the movie *Bullet to the Brain*. He also filmed the movie *Road to Paloma*, in which he starred. The movie was co-written and directed by Jason while also featuring Lisa Bonet.

2014 - He decided to try a new genre and acted in Debug, a horror-thriller movie. Jason also took the role of Philip Kopus in the movie The Redline and appeared in two episodes of Drunk TV. He also starred in the movie Wolves.

2016 - He made his Aquaman debut in 2016, *Batman vs Superman: Dawn of Justice*, where he made a cameo appearance. He also starred in the Netflix series *Frontier* as Declan Harp, playing the lead role. Also in *Once upon a Time in Venice*, he played the role of Spyder, a drug lord. Jason was published on the front page of Wednesday's edition of *USA Today* while talking about "Water and Sustainability." He played the role of Joe Bright in *Sugar Mountain* and Miami man in *The Bad Batch*.

2017 - He joins the Justice League team as Aquaman. Jason also was nominated for the Canadian Screen Awards for Best Actor in a Continuing Leading Dramatic Role for his movie *Frontier*. Jason also got married to his long-time crush Lisa Bonet.

2018 - Jason goes on to play Joe Braven in the movie *Braven* and also plays the character of Authur Curry in the DC movie *Aquaman*.

2019 - Jason plays the voice actor of Aquaman in the movie The Lego Movie 2: The Second Part. He also appeared in Season 31 of The Simpsons and played one of the leading roles in the Apple TV series See. The movie was nominated for IGN's Best Action Series of 2019. He raised a total of $31,000 thanks to the support of Ellen Degeneres's friends at Shutterfly for his charity course. The money was for Sustainable Coastlines Hawaii. Jason was nominated for the Nickelodeon Kids Choice Awards twice, MTV and Movie Awards, and also Teens Choice Awards for his movie Aquaman.

2020 - Jason produces a documentary on Native Americans trying to recover their foodways. It won Best Documentary Feature at the Red Nation Film Festival Awards in 2020 and received many positive reviews.

2021 - He played the role of Aquaman in Zack Snyder's Justice League and also played the role of Duncan Idaho in Dune. Jason also co-produced and starred in the movie Sweet Girl, playing the role of Ray Cooper.

2022 - Jason would be playing the role of Flip in his upcoming Netflix movie *Slumberland*.

"Jason Momoa" by Gage Skidmore is licensed under CC BY-SA 2.0.

References

Introduction

https://www.instyle.com/celebrity/jason-momoa-dune-interview-2020

https://www.boredpanda.com/jason-momoa-leica-cameras-collection/?utm_source=google&utm_medium=organic&utm_campaign=organic

https://www.jasonmomoanews.com/guinness-beer-jason-momoa/

Early Career

https://www.cheatsheet.com/entertainment/model-of-the-year-how-jason-momoa-lied-his-way-into-show-business.html/

Game of Thrones

https://www.cheatsheet.com/entertainment/jason-momoa-says-he-couldnt-get-work-after-game-of-thrones-we-were-starving.html/

Aquaman

https://www.cinemablend.com/news/2462374/jason-momoa-thought-he-was-up-for-a-dc-villain-during-his-aquaman-audition

https://www.cinemablend.com/news/1724049/why-jason-momoa-was-hired-as-aquaman-according-to-zack-snyder

https://ew.com/movies/2018/07/19/jason-momoa-aquaman-interview/

Jason Momoa hosts SNL

https://www.mensjournal.com/entertainment/jason-momoa-is-pumped-to-host-snl-in-these-

hilarious-videos/amp/

Snyder's Cut

https://collider.com/snyder-cut-ending-explained/

https://jxxspzd.com/justice-league-movie-snyder-cut-jason-momoa-reveals/

"FSC14 C3 su_0280" by Graffio! is licensed under CC BY-SA 2.0.

Final Surprise Bonus

Hope you've enjoyed this biography of Jason Momoa.

We always like to give more than we get, so I'd like to give you one final bonus.

Do me a favor, if you enjoyed this book, *please* leave a review on Amazon.

It'll help get the word out so more kids can find out more about Jason Momoa!

If you do, I'll send you one of my most cherished video collection – Free:

Ultimate Collection of Links to Jason Momoa's YouTube Videos!

You won't be able to say you know Ryan Reynolds until you watch these videos!